Seasons Poems

Compiled by John Foster

Contents

Acknowledgements

The Editor and Publisher wish to thank the following who have kindly given permission for the use of copyright material:

John Foster for 'Harvest time' and 'One summer evening' both © 1995 John Foster; Julie Holder for 'Seasons of trees' © 1995 Julie Holder; John Kitching for 'Here and there' © 1995 John Kitching; Wendy Larmont for 'Winter walk' © 1995 Wendy Larmont; Tony Mitton for 'Hibernating hedgehog' © 1994 Tony Mitton; Irene Rawnsley for 'Footprints' © 1995 Irene Rawnsley; Charles Thomson and John Foster for 'You can tell it's spring' © 1995 Charles Thomson and John Foster.

Seasons of trees

In spring
The trees
Are a beautiful sight
Dressed in blossom
Pink and white.

In summer
The trees
Are full of treats
Apples and pears
And cherries to eat.

In autumn
The trees
Are red and gold
And the leaves fall down
As the days grow cold.

In winter
The trees
Are bare and plain
Waiting for spring
To dress them again.

Julie Holder

3

Winter walk

Walking home from Granny's
On a dark and snowy night,
Everything looks ghostly
In the shadowy street light.

All is still and quiet.
No footsteps can be heard,
Except the crunch beneath us.
Too cold to say a word.

Wendy Larmont

4

Footprints

In the winter
watch me go,
making footprints
in the snow.

In the spring
my boots are wet.
See how deep
the puddles get.

6

In the summer
by the sea,
sandy footprints
made by me.

In the autumn
trees are brown.
I kick the leaves
all over town!

Irene Rawnsley

Here and there

There in Jamaica
The sun beats down.
Here the dark clouds
Fiercely frown.

There in Jamaica
Bright blue, warm.
Here huge snowflakes
Thickly swarm.

8

There in Jamaica
Storms whip trees.
Here frozen ponds,
Icy seas.

There in Jamaica
A sun-tan glow.
Here wrapped up tight
From top to toe.

John Kitching

Harvest time

Harvest time! Harvest time!
It's harvest time again.
Time to cut the corn
And gather in the grain.

Harvest time! Harvest time!
Time to pick the fruits,
To gather in the nuts
And dig up all the roots.

Harvest time! Harvest time!
In the autumn sun
We'll cut, pick and dig
Until the harvest's done.

John Foster

Hibernating hedgehog

Here comes winter,
cold and grey.
The hedgehog tucks
itself away.

Here comes ice
and here comes snow.
It needs somewhere
warm to go.

Here comes mist
and freezing fog.
Here's a good old
hollow log.

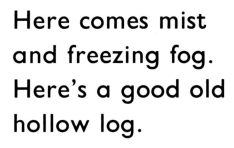

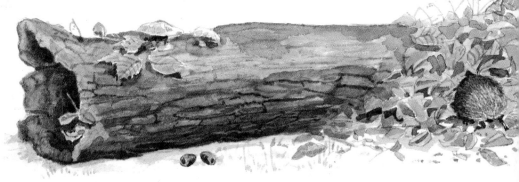

And here's a pile
of leaves that's deep.
It rolls up tight
and goes to sleep.

Tony Mitton

You can tell it's spring

You can tell it's spring
When the trees turn green
And there are just puddles
Where the snow has been.

You can tell it's spring
When the birds build nests
And Mum packs away
Our warm winter vests.

You can tell it's spring
When the yellow heads
Of daffodils dance
In the flower-beds.

You can tell it's spring.
It's lighter each day
And after school
We can stay out and play.

Charles Thomson and John Foster

15

One summer evening

We were playing cricket
in the garden after school.
Dad dived for a catch,
but he missed
and fell in the paddling pool!

John Foster

Printed in Hong Kong